LIFE'S MOSAIC

TANYA WHITE | Author

Cassandra Allen | Editor

Publisher Sadie Books, 215 East Camden Ave #G-2, Moorestown, NJ 08057 sadie-books.com
856-313-0548

ISBN # 978-0-9816047-9-4
Library of Congress Control # 2012951036

Cover Art/Interior/Exterior Layout callendesign.com
Cover Photography - Jonathon Bakan

Life's Mosaic is a collection of short contemplations and poems, which explore the varying experiences that encompass this play that we call life. One takes a journey into different worlds through the author's brush stroke, illuminating different landscapes of reality. We explore every imaginable theme, from the nuances of love and sexual expression to the struggles and simplistic joys of life, as well as delving into the depth of the spiritual journey to discover the truth of our divine nature.

The reader soars through different dimensions, stretching beyond the limiting confines of the mind, and is encouraged to contemplate the source of all creation. Yet the author does not disregard the human expression of life's journey. The author gives readers erotic injections of poems that invite one's senses to erupt in pleasure, and moments to sit with the common challenges we face as human beings. At the end of each subtopic are pages to diary one's thoughts as they relate to each subject. In these particular sections, one is encouraged to journal about emotional, cognitive, spiritual and ultimately transformative life experiences he or she encounters while personally delving deeply into the meaning of the contemplations. Perceive the diary as an alive, engaging process of exploration of your being as it relates to the topic of discussion.

So, one can say that Life's Mosaic attempts to give the reader a direct experience of the diversity of the soul's journey in this plane of human existence. It is an attempt to shine the light on the varying costumes of reality that we wear as spiritual beings having a human experience. In its' truest essence, Life's Mosaic is a genuine attempt to reveal the illusion of the physical realm. Although all of our experiences may feel and appear to be the totality of truth as we know it in any given moment, readers are encouraged to merge into the fluidity of our lives, causing them to give pause and consider that there's more to every experience than meets the limited perception of the human eye.

Yes, there are many flavors within this work called Life's Mosaic that are sure to tickle the reader's palate, and hopefully begin to stretch and loosen consolidated, rigid beliefs and ideas embedded in each of us regarding who we "think" ourselves to be.

DEDICATED TO MY MOTHER

JULIA LENETTA WHITE

08/09/1951- 12/20/1979

WHOSE JOURNEY WAS FAR TOO SHORT

MY MOTHER'S SMILE

My mother's smile... If I could just see it once more

Not that I remember it for sure,

But my mother's smile,

Somehow, I know that if she could,

She would just hold me in her arms another moment.

Perhaps just a knock at the crown of her heart could have erased the pain she felt...

My mother's smile, when she had one, could make anyone's heart melt.

My mother's smile was filled with sugar and spice and, yeah, some things that weren't so nice.

My mother's smile... Who knows what it stole to keep the blood coursing through her veins?

My mother's smile lives on in me... today let it rain.

Let her reign...

ABOUT THE AUTHOR

Tanya White has written since she was a young child. Born and raised in an inner city, impoverished neighborhood within SE Washington, D.C, her world drastically changed when she lost her mother to suicide at the age of eight, and began a life of living in foster and group homes.

As a young teenage girl of 13, she auditioned and qualified for entry to the prestigious high school of performing arts, Duke Ellington School of the Arts, in Washington, D.C. Upon completing high school, she attended the University of the Arts in Philadelphia, Pennsylvania, where she studied classical voice. Following her studies as a voice major, Ms. White completed her Bachelors of Science degree in Nursing at Howard University in Washington D.C., and she subsequently obtained her Masters of Social Work Degree from Temple University in Philadelphia, Pennsylvania.

Throughout her years as a performer, and now as a Registered Nurse in Hospice Care and alternative healing, she has continued to develop her craft as a writer, never losing her passion for the written word. Ms. White has utilized writing as an avenue to express the often-burgeoning emotions and feelings within her being and heart. Her intention is to touch others and ignite in them that which enlivens them and causes them to re-embrace their life's journey with zest and fervor!

Contact Tanya White:

Loveheals1@yahoo.com

https://www.facebook.com/LifesMosaic

TABLE OF CONTENTS

III. FROM THE HUMAN TO THE DIVINE

UNIVERSAL CALLING

Home

NOISINESS OF THE PERSONALITY

Breath

NOWHERE TO JOURNEY

Touch God

RELIGION

Essence

IN THE STATE OF NO MIND

SEEKER

No Words Needed

EXPERIENCE YOUR TRUE SELF

I. OUR SHARED HUMANITY

THE PERFECT LIFE... ???

Is there such a thing as a perfect life? I sit and revel in this question. If I were to ask you, "What is a perfect life?" most may reply that it is one without suffering, perhaps with a variation or two thrown in for idealistic measure. However, for the most part, I think it is safe to assume that most of us simply want to be happy, with next to none or as minimal as possible suffering.

Ok, let us go with this as our philosophical base. Based on this common assumption that "We all want to be happy", we can then move forward and say the determination of happiness varies tremendously from one to the next in the spectrum of human expression. Personal life experiences, from lifetimes before, form our individual perceptions of life and this world, and color our human lenses. Imprints forge in the delicacy of our soul's marrow as we incubate in the warmth of our mother's womb. Although we may not have a cognizance of being in the womb, I do believe karmic wiring is laid, even before we release our first cry, announcing our arrival into this world.

Given these underpinnings, what would you suppose is a perfect life? If we accept the presumption that living in this university called *life* is predisposed to our karmic retribution, as well as whatever lessons life throws into the mix, can there ever be such a thing as a perfect life?

Many of us have been guilty of comparison-shopping in regards to eyeing other's lives and comparing them to our own. We readily make lists of all that we are enamored with about a particular person's life. In my own case, I have heard others express to me on numerous occasions, any myriad of adorations, from "Oh my gosh! You're a nurse...wow! You're so lucky!" They are never the wiser that I feel trapped by nursing, often seeing it as my only means of making a living because I have done it for the past 16 years now! Or, "Wow, that is so amazing - all of the traveling you do. It must be nice not to have children. If I did not have so many responsibilities with my kids and family, I would travel the world like you! One day maybe..." They are, again, none the wiser that I long to have a family of my own. The thirst I have for a sense of belonging is raging in me on a daily basis. Having had no parents and growing up in foster care, I have struggled for years to fill the void within me from lack of family.

Therefore, you see it is all in our perception. Speaking of which, this just occurred to me. Perhaps a life without suffering is not the "perfect life" after-all. Let us change it up for a moment and surmise that we can expect some level of discomfort, from time to time, in life. We cannot avoid it, so better to embrace it. In that embracing, we can say that suffering then becomes optional, sort of like laughter through tears.

'What do I mean by that?' you ask.

Somehow, if we can begin to loosen our demand that we experience only pleasure, then perhaps we will begin to free ourselves from our frozen expectations of life. Living within the confines of a paradigm that life only expresses in certain ways outlined on our "do's and don't" lists creates stagnancy and deadness. What if we could allow the vibrancy of being present in the moment, impacted by the powerful energetic nuances of our interactions with one another, to ignite a fuller and richer quality of living? We can make a choice in how we meet the experiences we have in any given moment. While that experience may indeed be painful, it does not have to include suffering. Suffering occurs when we are resistant to what is. It occurs when we say..NO! This is not what is supposed to be happening! I want this instead. Furthermore, while caught in the grips of protesting a "thing", strife and SUFFERING occur as a result.

Nevertheless, if we simply allow the experience, WHATEVER it may be, to wash through us like a fresh, falling, summer rain... aahhh, then, in that moment, we will realize the perfection in life's imperfection. Could it have been designed any other way? Hhmm... I feel not.

You're Beautiful

You're beautiful... you're beautiful

Just as you are

Even with flaws, unfinished promises and bruises left from your childhood years.

Still, your beauty prevails.

The hole left when the woman who gave birth to you took a self-imposed early exit from this physical realm,

Has been filled by many human angels, along the way.

They've been a blessing to you, I must say

To that lost child hidden in an adult woman's body,

Hidden behind the smile that has been plastered on her face from day to day

Hiding the pains, so deathly afraid that she would break!

Especially if they really knew the deepest secret she hides,

The one that flashes with constant thoughts of how to fly

Away to heaven and sit in the lap of her Savior held tight in his arms for eternity!

But not yet....

It's just not meant to be

Because you see

She has a mission that was laid before time became a notion

It's all about love and unending devotion

Devotion to spread the warmth of the truth to other children who, like her, have been abused

Who like her have been used.

Who like her have longed to truly be seen!

Who like her wished for the perfect dream to manifest of a father.

And a mother, who would hold her tenderly to her soft breasts,

Singing sweet lullabies at night when she was laid to rest

No matter how distant or long ago those brutal memories are...

She's still carrying the scar

Buried deep within the folded sheets and layers of her soul.

But, all it took was for her to be told just once

You're Beautiful!

You're Beautiful!!

You're Beautiful!!!

DIARY NOTES

DIARY NOTES

_____

_____

_____

_____

_____

_____

_____

_____

_____

_____

_____

_____

DIARY NOTES

DIARY NOTES

LOSS

Often when we talk about loss, we conjure up thoughts of the people we have lost to death, or relationships that have ended, romantic ones and friendships, perhaps loss of a physical ability or dexterity due to illness or some unimaginable trauma of which we are victims. With those losses comes the experience of pain, sorrow, grief. I am no stranger to loss in my life, from all of the categories listed above, with perhaps the exception of a major physical disadvantage for which I am deeply grateful. As I reflected back over the various losses that I have experienced over the brief span of my 42 years on this planet, one thing stood out to me, glaring, almost blinding me with the purity of its truth. And that is --- in the midst of the fire of those losses , the subsequent tears shed and pain felt, was a profound center, a still point, where all else fell away and I simply was.

To describe this state as peace-filled does not do it justice. Yes, peace was present, but there was also a sense of being brand-new in my Spirit. Yet, it was not new at all, it was more of a coming home, a state of resting in the depth of the Self. I do not want to give the fairytale illusion that the process of going through the fire of the grief was not arduous, and at times tortuous to my heart in ways that words fail to describe. No, it was hell! I do not want to mislead you in any way. Additionally, during that all-consuming hell, a force saturated the pain, stripping me of the layers of trauma, grief and disappointments that had covered over my soul throughout the years. Dare I say - the pain was washing, nourishing, transforming me?

So, what have I learned from these experiences of loss, you ask. I am learning that through direct experience and submersion, rather than avoidance of and denial of whatever grief we may experience during any type of loss, we dissolve yet another layer of that which keeps us from our true selves. We melt another layer of the ego.

Recently, I learned of the process of how a pearl becomes a pearl. The oyster, in its shell, because of some piece of sand irritating it, begins to release a substance, which engulfs the piece of sand, hardens and crystallizes it, thus, becoming a pearl. What a beautiful analogy, I thought, for our experiences of loss. Yes, it is extremely painful, and at times, we may even feel that we are at our breaking point; the pain is so great! Then, watch what happens! Like the oyster, our soul releases its healing balm through our tears, guttural sobs and cries, engulfing and surrounding that which we no longer need. It purges all of our accumulated, false identifications and attachments to who we thought ourselves to be prior to the experience of that loss. In the intense fire of our burned egos, we emerge as the true pearls, which we are in the depth of our being. We emerge as Moses did when he came down from having talked with God in the burning bush, more radiant and vibrant, Full of our Divine Light.

Therefore, embrace life's painful experiences - all of them, not just the major ones mentioned above, but also losses of who we thought we and others were. This includes loss of a dream that did not manifest the way we thought it would; and/or loss of your favorite eight-track tape that was of sentimental value because your dad gave it to you in 1972 - whatever it may be. Face it! Meet it head on. Try your hardest not to run from it. Because in running, you avoid the Pearl of you.

Loss Touched Me Deep

Ahhhhh...I can't breathe another moment of this grief that leaves me blinded and unable to see my path.

My head is spinning; my chest is aching, bending under its familiar grasp

How many times have I been told that time heals all wounds?

But, no one has spoken away my pain.

Time must have a slow refrain.

Next to the empty hole, left in my heart, where your presence used to sparkle,

Is the ravaged sore of a distant memory lost through all the echoes of feelings I have felt in time immemorial

I have no more to offer

My cup runneth over and out of sustenance that gives me life...

Tears I can cry no more, because it leaves me feeling empty and torn...

Never before has there been a story told quite like mine...

Yes.....

I know... I know... I have to be grateful because somewhere in the Netherlands lies a withered butterfly...whose cry has gone unheard...

Somewhere there's a motherless child longing for just one word of comfort and a soft touch against her cheek.

Then there are also the meek

Who never complain, but endure life's pain

And continue to walk with heads held high.

Then why oh why!!

Does my heart seem to have no reprieve?

From the dreary lull, that keeps me on bended knee

Asking for a break from the tempestuous droll of another day

Yes, it may all sound insane...

But trust that every man, woman, boy and girl

have traveled through this

Dark night of which I speak

It's just that some may not have been touched

By loss engrained so deep.....

AS I...

How Do I?

How does one express, find the words to say...

"My heart-light has been dimmed" when someone he or she loves has crossed back to spirit.

How do you find the place inside to gather the strength to say, "I am still breathing in this physical body?"

Although, you are not.

How do you nourish and soothe the tender spot that once filled with joy and laughter... how?

You may say that we all have a date with death, or they are in a better place.

Yes, you may even say that there but for the Grace...

Ooohhh, how I've heard those words a thousand times!

But somehow.... there.... right there in the midst, I can still see you smile..:)

I can still hear your voice.

I can still feel your touch.

I had more things to share with you...

I wanted to know and merge with you deeper still.

I wanted to let you into the crevices of my soul that had yet to be touched...

But, I feared...

Feared this love I felt for you couldn't be real

Feared your angelic presence was a mirage ...birthed from my ever-present dream state

And now.... Fate

Fate has rung her ominous bell and silence replaces the familiar melodious sound of your voice.

I enter into the only place I know you remain

The only place where I can still hear you call my name

The only place where I have a chance to remain sane!

The place where you and I held secret

ceremonies and whispered love stories never told.

The place where I still give you my hand like a tiny child to hold...

I enter into my heart and know that when I do

You will meet me there and I,

Once again,

Will FEEL you say ....

I LOVE YOU.

DIARY NOTES

_____

_____

_____

_____

_____

_____

_____

_____

_____

_____

_____

_____

DIARY NOTES

DIARY NOTES

DIARY NOTES

FEAR

Fear is a shared common human experience, one with which every human being on the planet is familiar. Fear, in and of itself, is not a "bad thing". The body spontaneously undergoes a visceral experience in response to a situation. Now, here comes the complicated piece, belief/thought. This is where fear becomes problematic; it gets married to thought.

Let us pause right here. Consider for a moment your number one fear. What lurks in the recesses of your mind and causes you unrest? We all have that one, two or three core fears, realistic or not, that have set up camp in the matrix of our being. It never quite leaves us. In insidious ways, it shows up in our lives in varying disguises, causing havoc and discontentment. Its food is the continuous stream of thoughts we streamline into our consciousness.

At a certain point, the immediate danger, if one was present to begin with, has dissolved, and all that remains is a nebulous, self-created, fear-ridden monster. Now, that is not to say that experiences do not lend themselves to the creation of this monster. We may have had many unpleasant experiences that have aided in solidifying whatever false, core beliefs we carry that aids in replenishing the life of our "main" fear projection.

Perhaps we've had experiences where our confidence and trust in others has been undermined time and time again; or we have faced abandonment during times of greatest need in our lives; or been abused emotionally, physically, or both - the list that we can generate is endless, I'm sure. The question is, "do these experiences, and subsequent beliefs we develop about them, have a life of their own"? Or, can they only survive with our continued belief and active streaming of energy into them?

I am beginning to know the truth of experiencing the deflation of fear when I, with awareness, withdraw fear's life supply, which is that of thought. The mind is exceptionally powerful, because it is consciousness in essence. It is God in contracted form. It simply has forgotten its true nature. How powerful is 'thought'? A thought, if followed through, can set one on an angry rampage, or into a creative, dizzy spell of spontaneous service to others! It can make one feel as if he or she is a queen or king sitting on top of the world or the lowest scum of the earth. Correction, it is not the thought itself that does this. Energy of our belief in that thought does. A thought can come in and go out of our minds swiftly! Alternatively, it can set up residence, get comfortable, linger and fester... building, getting fatter, more engorged until it is a fear-ridden demon that has nothing but suffering in store for us.

So, now that we have explored the origins, growth and viability of "fear", one may ask, what do we do about it?! Well, it seems to me, a good starting point is the interruption of its food source... thought; and, more importantly, our belief and attachment to the thought. We have to test the waters of those hidden, core beliefs buried deep within our sub-conscious and challenge them. In challenging them, we will see them disappear like vapors in the wind! They are not real! They are illusory! They exist only because we give them permission and continuously keep them alive by our fierce belief in them.

Nevertheless, do not take my word for it. Let me offer an experiment of sorts. The next time you feel a familiar sense of fear rising within you concerning a hard-wired core belief that you carry, take a deep breath, see the "thought" that has arrived for its habitual visit, welcome it, **fully acknowledge** it, then say goodbye to it and send it on its way. Let the emptiness that follows its departure grow; and find that all that remains is a sense of empty, pristine, clear spaciousness. In that moment, perhaps the visceral tightness, heart palpations, as well as any other sensations you were aware of, may have left along with that thought. Then I want you to do something really important!!! I want you to consciously, with as much awareness as you can muster, observe your current experience and ask yourself what is the truth of it. Is what I feared present here in this situation? Oftentimes, we will be surprised to discover that the answer is 'no'! Not only is it 'no', it is oftentimes the complete opposite of the very thing we feared.

Now, that is not to say that there will not be moments when the answer will be 'yes'. I know, bummer! In those instances, the important thing to remember is that we have the power to choose our reaction to our thoughts. Do not try to pretend that fear is not present, or ignore it, while there is a thought waging a nasty war against your fledgling attempt to hold onto one semblance of sanity in the moment! No, again, welcome it, recognizing that it is not the totality of your experience. It is only a fleeting, temporary blip on the radar of your life. It will pass just in the same manner that it arrived.

This phenomenon of fear is not so scary when we begin to recognize that it gains power from our belief in our thoughts about life situations. How liberating is that! It cannot exist without our active engagement in nourishing it, no matter what is unfolding before us in any given moment. I do not know about you, but I derive tremendous hope, lightness of being, and happiness in knowing that.

Blessings and Light to us on this journey.... SoHam.

I Can't Breathe...

My breath is in a chokehold, stuck in a relentless barrage of incessant anxiety.

I want to reach out and ask for help, but to whom can I turn?

I can't say what's inside of me, words fail to describe the all-encompassing paralysis of life's pulsation

Frozen am I, in a space without time

Today, I can't breathe!

I feel like I'm struggling to find hope.

Today I can't breathe!

My breath is stuck on the bridge linking here to nowhere.

Looking around at all the people moving, living their lives in fast forward motion,

While I stand still, frozen in Fear.

I feel lost!

Enveloped in pain-stained walls of an invisible prison

From which I can't break free!

I try everything, everything!!!

I push and push,

Trying to maintain hope that somehow the next moment will kiss me with lips free from the hammering of my racing heartbeat resounding in my ears

Oh but then another day arrives, and the shell remains unbroken

And still.........I can't breathe...

Can anyone rescue me from this holographic hell, cluttered with constant worries and disasters yet to unfold

I am trapped,

There is no way out!

Death is a welcome friend, but so far out of reach!!

That's the only thing I can see that will set me free,

Because today I can't breathe...

DIARY NOTES

DIARY NOTES

DIARY NOTES

DIARY NOTES

II. LOVE, SEX AND THE IN BETWEEN

WHAT IS LOVE?

Is it a tangible object? No. Yet some of us witness it. It seems love is a feeling/energy, which occurs within our spaciousness of being, just as other emotions come and go. I remember having a particular experience with someone that, on a personality level, I did not like. She and I did not get along. Truthfully, she despised me more than I did her. I primarily hated the harmful, energetic arrows she would throw my way, anytime we interacted with one another. My personality struggled tremendously with not being "liked". Anyway, I digress.

This person and I were sitting face-to-face having a conversation one particular day, during a workshop in the healing school we attended. As we were talking, in an instant - a blink of an eye - my heart cracked wide open (and I say 'heart' because I do not have another word to describe from whence this pure feeling of bliss and love ascended). Everything fell away. All thoughts, judgments and history between she and I ceased to exist in that moment. Even the physical parameters of where my body ended and hers began did not exist. Actually, I experienced myself as space. Yet, something had to be aware of witnessing this unfolding, or there would be no memory for me to call upon to describe it.

Therefore, I can say that love is energy. This is the

only word that I have in my 'direct' knowing to describe it. It is one-step removed from the purity of consciousness, and yet is composed of the essence of consciousness. Yet, unlike other emotions and feelings that arise within our vast spaciousness of being, I feel it is the only one that is devoid of labels, conditioning, attachments, judgments, mental distortions and other constructs of the mind that take form. Nonetheless, we can witness and experience it. So, contrary to what I formerly used to rattle off like a parrot, ("We are love") because it was what I had been taught, it cannot be the final say of who I am, simply because "who I am" is witnessing this experience of love.

Yet in the same breath, we can say that perhaps the experience of love's energy, arising within that vast space that we are, is the closest we will come, within the context of duality, to knowing the taste of our true nature. When the mind, and therefore, duality and our sense of being this "person", is completely absorbed back into spaciousness (consciousness), no constructs or energies, including the highest, most undiluted of them 'Love', exists as a separate experience being had and therefore, witnessed. We are that which is unknown as an experience or phenomena. It is similar to how a pen cannot write itself. Experiences arise and take shape within the infinite, giving us an objectified knowing of self, including the experience of Love.

When I Say I Do

When I say I do...

With all that is within me from this life and the others on rewind,

I will pledge to you

All that I am, the good and the ever changing for better,

To be your anchor in all kinds of weather,

To ride waves of laughter and tears in the same fashion,

To hold and cherish your heart with the tenderness you so deserve,

Never to disturb the delicate balance of what you have so freely given me,

Your heart, your soul, your dreams, and your tender spots

Unhidden, yes, revealed for me to see,

I promise you when I say I do with excitement, longing, passion, vulnerability, and yes, Love burgeoning in my soul,

I will inhale you into my being

And, in that moment...we will arrive

Home

What If...?

What if we could kiss each other's souls?

What if when we touched, this bodily form melted away

And all that was left in its wake

Was our essence?

Could you still find me amongst the crowd?

Would you recognize my timber and the nuances of my being?

How they harmonize with yours

What if we had no body but could touch each other so deeply

We had no sense of separation?

No ending ... no beginning.

Would you still feel my caress?

I want to know you like this

So, when the form falls away, or withers

Into some ill- mannered, disguise of the 'you'

My eyes first beheld,

My heart would not miss a beat in continuing to lavish you

With sweet lullabies.

I want to share butterfly kisses with no eyelashes left to flutter.

Know me from this space without time.

Then and only then, will we know the depth of Heart's Purest Love,

Not determined by how fine she is, or other empty, hollowed out

Mutterings of the wiles of the mind!

Can you feel me?

Then know this...

I see you without eyes needed!

I breathe in the aroma of you, without needing to take a breath.

Your taste saturates my being

I feel your touch without skin because you

caress the marrow of my soul

And I heard you coming, long before you
arrived...

DIARY NOTES

DIARY NOTES

_____

_____

_____

_____

_____

_____

_____

_____

_____

_____

_____

_____

_____

DIARY NOTES

DIARY NOTES

TWO-YEAR MOMENT OF TEMPORARY INSANITY

Over and over and over and over again, I repeated the same actions, and felt the same longing deep in my heart for connection with someone that simply **could not, would not and was deathly afraid of opening to love.**

I ask myself now, what the hell was wrong with you?!! Why did you keep reaching out to someone who repeatedly slapped your hand away?! I get it, you could not let go of the first weekend you spent with her; the way she looked into your eyes as you lay face to face on the couch, whispering the words forever seared into your heart. "So, what do you need? What do you want?" The melodious sound of her voice sauntered through her disarming, sweet smile, dancing slowly in your ears. Now that I hear those words on rewind, I realize that was my first clue that this would be an unhealthy, co-dependent, hell of an emotional, roller-coaster ride.

Never once did I stop to think that my wound of needing to feel a sense of belonging, connection and being loved, was hooking directly into her need and pattern of care-taking others. It was a perfect puzzle - fit.......**literally!** That is until the puzzle edges started to fray and I realized my pieces were not a match for her world after all.

However, as is the nature of unhealthy life patterns, I kept banging, reshaping, trying from a different angle to make my puzzle pieces fit hers. I need her, I told myself. I want her, I whispered. The angel in the other realm of my conscious mind had even convinced me that I was in love with her!! **Wow......**

The mind can take you on a toxic trip filled with happily ever after, fairytale fantasies layered with mystical delusions of grandeur; all the while keeping reality shrouded in a dark blanket of denial. The signs were all there and all pervasive. She had a partner. She showed me and told me in various ways that she would never jeopardize the only family she had, that of her partner and her mom. I did not listen. I chose rather to focus on the emotional breadcrumbs she randomly scattered along the way, paving an elusive trail that kept me attached and frustrated.

Why was I frustrated you ask? Because I always wanted more, more than she would ever have the capacity to give me. I do believe what I stirred in her scared the shit out of her! I do believe that the connection we shared when we first met caught her off guard. I do believe that she was unprepared for the line that we crossed. I believe if life circumstances were different, perhaps the two-year emotionally draining, life sucking, tug of war push-and-pull of, "Come close, no go away!" may have unfolded differently, undoubtedly.

But...my puzzle pieces didn't fit hers...

And, I finally have the courage to realize and accept..

They never will....

DIARY NOTES

_____

_____

_____

_____

_____

_____

_____

_____

_____

_____

_____

_____

DIARY NOTES

DIARY NOTES

DIARY NOTES

SEXUAL HEALING

Sex....say the word and it conjures up a myriad of emotions, thoughts, and bodily sensations. It is the most potent word in the human language that can invoke a response that runs the full spectrum of human expression from passion, desire, disdain, anger, and frustration to bliss.

Let us have an open dialogue about sex and sexual energy, and discuss the different distortions assigned to it throughout the years. Many have come to relate to sex within our culture as being taboo, considered something that one does in the privacy of his or her home, whether with one's self or another. While we have progressed in our understanding and embracing of sexuality, say since the time of Ozzie and Harriet, when sex was not even a word that one could mutter, there are still huge misconceptions and stagnated structures that imprison our sexual energy.

Sexual energy is life-force energy. It originates from the same source (consciousness), as do all other creative energies that animate our existence as human beings in this play of life. Why then do we saddle the term 'sex' with negative labels such as "Eeew, they doin' the NASTY", for example? Why do we feel that sex is something dirty, or in some way "bad" inherently? Some would argue that these distortions around sex and sexual expression originate from a puritanical, religious ideology. Fundamentalist Christians have long espoused the rule that sexual copulation can only occur within the "sanctity" of marriage, between a man and a woman, for the sole purpose of procreation, not pleasure. This definition, therefore, does not include individuals of same sex orientation. Not to mention, most traditional Christian faiths deem homosexuality as an abomination. Although many Christians have resolved within themselves, over recent years, that they are perfect in the eyes of their creator. Therefore, they are not an abomination if *they* love the same sex!

Thus, one can see how a very natural, organic aspect of our human expression has become "dirtied" from man's interjection of certain philosophical beliefs and judgments. However, the natural energy of sexual desire and the expression and sharing of said desire with one another is pure and untainted. There is nothing "wrong" with sex, period. If it were not for sex, none of us would be here...double period!!

Now, I do not have my head in the sand in terms of not recognizing how some misuse sex, whether it is a form of addiction used to camouflage someone's deeper issues surrounding fear of true intimacy, or God forbid, when sex is used as a form of abuse. I am not referring to these ill-adjusted misuses of that which is an organic, creative force within us when I discuss sex as not being inherently bad. Face it; there will always be those who find unhealthy ways to use **anything**, when they are ill adjusted mentally and emotionally.

So, please let us not go on the tangent of that conversation of how sex can be unhealthy. **Anything** can be unhealthy, if used inappropriately. I am simply referring to sexual energy, (a form of life energy), in its un-manipulated expression. When sexual juices, so to speak, receive full permission to express, surge, and spill over within our being, it enhances every aspect of our lives. It enhances our physical well-being due to the rush of feel-good endorphins, which reenergizes us emotionally and spiritually.

Now, the opposite can be true when we decidedly sever that very beautiful aspect of ourselves. When we abstain from sexual copulation, whether with another or ourselves (masturbation... yaaayyy!), we sever our life force. We sever a deeper connection with lovers and ourselves. Frustration, irritability, deadening of our creative flow and self-expression are all negative by-products of denying our sexual energy free expression. Bathing our nerve endings with the lush bounty of endorphins that release when one marinates in sexual energy, not to mention when one reaches the pinnacle of an orgasm, can be extremely healing. Sex can foster a deeper sense of intimacy with our mate/mates and ourselves. It can serve as a doorway to freeing up energetic and emotional blocks that hold us prisoner and prevent us from expressing ourselves fully. There are gifts that lie in embracing our sexual life energy...many, many gifts.

Hence, today I challenge the old paradigm that lingers that considers sex to be "naughty", "nasty", and any other word the human mind has painted with its contorted brush. I encourage each of us to reclaim our sexual life. **Relish it! Enjoy it! Savor it!** When and if it falls away, let it do so in its own timing, **naturally**, which, by the way, occurs as well. However, I prefer celibacy as a natural unfolding rather than something forced in the name of **ANY** religious or philosophical ideal. Those ideals are merely as we discussed in earlier conversations, thoughts. In addition, those thoughts only gain power from our subsequent belief in them. Without our imbuing them with energy, they fade like ethers in the mist.

So, again, dance upon the luscious waves of your sexual (life force) energy pulsating within your being, and meet yourself in ecstasy!

Orgasm

Oh God....

I'm bout to.....

Explode from this mind blowing sensation that is rocking

My body with wave after wave of

Cataclysmic Vibrations!

Leaving my breath on pause....

As my heart is desperately trying to maintain its pace

But slowly losing the race

Against the creamy flow making its way down my inner thighs

Heading south into my lover's

Mouth that is watering at the mere

Drop of my nectar so sweet.

Dipping your element into the depths of

My unearthed nature

As you begin to feel the tumultuous pulsations

Of the culmination of that wild ride!

You know...

The one where I rode you up and down!

Feeling the motions

of your strong rod

Strokin'

Hittin' my spot.. so hot

Never losin' rhythm...Aii Dios Mio

You had me swimmin', beggin' for sweet release!!

As you thrust into me with the power of a lion's stance

Dammm!! You're a Mutha*&%$ Beast!!

As you tightly grasp my hips and suckle at my breast tips

Yes...you have my permission to continue to feast.

Just a little to the right,

aaiii now to the left...

What are you doing to me, this is insane!!

I bet the "Neighbors Know My Name"

There's just no way

I can hold back the passion coursing through my veins.

Aii..don't stop...please don't stop

I'm on the verge.....

Of the most amazing, soul wrenching, blazin'

Orgasm.....

You heard....

DIARY NOTES

DIARY NOTES

DIARY NOTES

DIARY NOTES

III. FROM THE HUMAN TO THE DIVINE

UNIVERSAL CALLING

I do not know the specific details of each of your life stories with its' joys and pains. However, one thing I know is that we are each a unique manifestation of the Divine, of Consciousness. Somehow, through experiencing the duality of this physical plane of existence, we have developed amnesia and fallen into a deep slumber, completely oblivious to the truth of who we are. It is as if someone sprinkled fairy dust in our eyes and we became spellbound by this world and our existence as this person. So much of our energy goes to the pursuit of discovering our "calling". We think about it day in and day out. We exhaust ourselves mentally and emotionally, trying to determine and even create something in which we can finally say "Aha! I found it...and here it is. **THIS** is my **CALLING**!" Consider for a moment, there is nothing to do. Yes, I know this goes contrary to everything we have been taught to believe. Let me try to take what I am stating to a fuller understanding.

We are that greater intelligence that holds every action and reaction, every thought, emotion, feeling, and sensation within its bosom; these are all phenomena spontaneously arising within you...the Self, the soul, consciousness, the Divine being that we are. If it were not so, then when that intelligent, all knowing force left the physical body at the time of "death", the body would remain animated and functioning, radiant and full of life. So at least we can agree that we are not this body/mind. If we are not the body/mind, and we agree that we are a Divine being, let's say (although words fail to fully describe who we are), then we can trust that everything that unfolds within this play that we call reality, will unfold organically, spontaneously, without any coercion needed from the level of our personalities/minds.

Now, I am not saying that you can't participate in the practical level of planning and organizing, (sending invites to a fundraiser; buying toys for tots or furniture for a group home; making phone calls to raise money for that group home, etc.) to manifest a desire within your heart. I do offer, however, that life is unfolding naturally of its' own accord. If it naturally occurs to you to feed the poor, you will find yourself in that action. The being that you are, life itself, will unfold in such a way that you find yourself in the action of preparing food and delivering it to the homeless. If it feels natural to sing, your mouth will open, and sound in the form of a song will arise. Life is unfolding without any planning in the way that we have learned it, needing to happen. Perhaps the more we trust that our innate, true nature is all-knowing, the less we are confused, misdirected and snared by our mind's ramblings. More peace will ensue because of this, because we are no longer struggling from an egoic state to determine a calling for ourselves. We are moving with the natural flow of the life force that we are; and in that movement, we can experience everything, knowing that it is transpiring within our very own being.

I previously held a strong belief and attachment to the concept that we are all here for a purpose and we all have a specific "calling". In addition, while I know it is a popular paradigm, in which others condition the vast majority of us to believe, consider for a moment that perhaps the highest "calling" we have in this journey of life has no personal agenda. It has no specific qualities, but rather a universal one and that is to come into directly experiencing the truth of who we are, a Divine being masquerading in a human play. Consider for a moment that all that unfolds in our lives is simply a part of the play that unfolds in its' variety and multi-colored labyrinth of plots and story lines. However, ultimately, I sense in my heart that the calling for each of us, if one exists in truth, is to realize our true Divine nature.

With that stated, this play is extremely seductive and powerful in its' allure. As a result, the divine being that we are, has gotten lost in its' own concoction that it brewed outside of the linear framework of time. The challenge we face is the tug of war between steeping ourselves in the presence that witnesses this play called life or being lured by the aroma of this illusory world of characters, themes and different experiences. There is a balance to it all, where one does not see the world and what appears to be real as something to avoid, but rather as something that is unfolding within the vastness of consciousness, (you and I). We are simply the detached witnesses of it all.

Our personal desires and agenda will begin to fade and dim. The spaciousness of being which one experiences when centered in the Real Self becomes more prevalent with each passing moment. While a sense of attachment may still exist for us as human beings to this earthly, physical manifestation, there is also a growing space between what appears to be "real" and the presence that holds it all. It is similar to the scene in the Wizard of Oz, when Dorothy and her motley crew of traveling companions discover that there is someone behind the curtain running the show. The only thing I disagree with in that pivotal moment of the movie is when he says, "Pay no attention to the man behind the curtain!" I say that the man behind the curtain is synonymous with our true being, The Divine Self, (without all the distorted beliefs that particular character in the movie held about himself); and the outward manifestations of his puppet string maneuverings. What we call reality is in fact the illusion. We need to turn our attention within to the all-pervasive, never-ending Self, which is pulling all the puppet strings to this very convincing play that we call life.

Here is to answering the **Universal Call** of awakening to our True Divine Self!

Home

It is said that God took form to experience itself

But then forgot itself in the play of its design

All day wandering in various human disguises

Merging into creative masks

Walking the endless labyrinth of

Its clever conception

Then came the call

First as a whisper

Floating like a silhouette upon

The fleeting, whimsical wings of the soul

"Come back"

"Come back"

"Come back"

Home

DIARY NOTES

DIARY NOTES

_____

_____

_____

_____

_____

_____

_____

_____

_____

_____

_____

_____

DIARY NOTES

DIARY NOTES

_____

_____

_____

_____

_____

_____

_____

_____

_____

_____

_____

_____

THE NOISINESS OF THE PERSONALITY

I once experienced a memory of noisiness of identification with the ego/personality. It was so subtle. The sensations, feelings, emotions, and thoughts that arose within my experience, in the moment, drowned out awareness of my Divine presence. I was wrapped up in a whirlwind of attraction to someone. Within a matter of a week, those feelings became non-attraction to that same person! Insane! My mind and emotions completely went along for the ride. Then one night, I sat in silence for some time, and within minutes, (perhaps more like an hour or so passed by), there was a profound sense of stillness that settled within my being, and "I" the Self with a capitol S was present and fully aware.

Here is what I know from that experience, when the mind/ego/personality, (all one and the same), is running the show, one's Being is very noisy! The sense of peace and alert, expanded presence that one is shrinks. In other words, the **awareness** of that larger presence that we are shrinks. Because the truth of who we are even holds the unfolding of the shrinking awareness, and therefore, can never itself shrink.

At times, I have heard myself talk about "my spiritual" path, as if it is a thing that is owned, and that I fit into my life. Many of us do this. We fit whatever ideology we "believe in" into our lives while concurrently continuing to live in ways that are totally ego-based. Christians may say it is like going to church on Sunday but the remainder of the week it is a free for all. The point that I am trying to interject here is that I no longer desire to walk a "spiritual path". Truth be told, I feel a call inside to abandon my ego to the flames and completely surrender what is left of what I perceive to be me, even the 'me' that thinks of her 'self' as a "spiritual seeker".

This has been the deepest lesson I have learned from my experience. Mental/emotional noise exists within the human realm. We cannot escape this realm. Consciousness took form and we are one of its' many expressions. Where I choose to direct my awareness and expend my energy will be toward realizing my true Self, beyond the many masks and roles that consciousness has assumed in this current incarnation. I thirst for that! I breathe/inhale the urge to realize our Divine nature, and completely merge into that universal being. All other desires are quickly fading....SoHam.

Breath

Its' texture is camouflaged in varying hues

Leaving one spinning in its mist

Dancing in its' vapors

Intoxicated by the hint of freshness left in its wake

Breath

Her rhythm falls and rises on the fluid arch of our

Bellies

Flowing through the hollowed halls of our nostrils, pausing before exiting into

The immensity of space

Lingering there perched on a tree branch

As it lifts the bird who has crested on the bend of its

Upward turn

Carrying it into flight

Breath

After a morning rain, it lies as the fresh mirage of misty fog

Hovering over the hills and the valleys below

Breath

Feel it warm the coolness of your cheek

And laugh through the tendrils of your hair

While taking a leisurely Sunday afternoon drive

On a backcountry dirt road

Invisible to the naked eye at times

It does take us by surprise

How nourishing and replenishing

And life sustaining it can be

To simply

Breathe.....ahhhhhh.......

DIARY NOTES

_____

_____

_____

_____

_____

_____

_____

_____

_____

_____

_____

_____

DIARY NOTES

DIARY NOTES

DIARY NOTES

NOWHERE TO JOURNEY

There is nowhere to progress, nothing to learn, nothing to discover. In the moments that "I" (used very loosely here) have directly experienced our divine nature, it has not been through an arduous, intellectual thought or analytical process in which I have discovered some new fact or insight about my personality. It has occurred spontaneously and without effort. There is only space. I feel no sense of a separate identity and often do not have a sense of having a body in those moments. Awareness is my name here. There is no desire for anything to be different, not even a thought of a desire is present. I would say peace is present; and while it does feel deeply restful, at some point, even the awareness of peace merges within me. My location of time falls away. The tension of needing to be or create something or some activity, some quality, withers away. Yet even within all of those descriptions, there is something present and aware of those descriptions.

The closest experience of realizing the Self happened when I was 7 years old. I had a moment (that stays with me to this day) of what I realize now was a direct experience of the Self, the consciousness that we all are. I was looking out of the bedroom window of the apartment that I shared with my mother, growing up. In a moment, everything - the buildings, church, bus stop across the street - all disappeared, and nothing remained but this brilliant, white, yellow light, and the sense of Being. That light permeated everything and everywhere. "I", (God), was everything and everywhere.

Since that time, I have had other tastes of the Self. The longing that continues to burn within me is to remain awake and permanently sustained within our true nature, when the next taste of the Self arises, rather than becoming seduced back into the dream of this reality and complete identification with this personality called, "Tanya". Each moment, the intoxication of the drug of this illusory world is wearing off.

Touch God

Listen...there is a whisper that speaks from the breath that flows from your belly....

Touch God

Speak..... for the mind cannot contemplate from where this essence arises

Touch God

No more doubt as to your true Divine nature...touching God

Perhaps there was a moment that you forgot your true heritage...that which is steeped in glorious hues of sublime light that dispels darkness...from the pit of your soul

Touch God!

Riding the wave of infinite bliss, turn your awareness within and remember....

Who you really are!

DIARY NOTES

DIARY NOTES

DIARY NOTES

DIARY NOTES

_____

_____

_____

_____

_____

_____

_____

_____

_____

_____

_____

RELIGION

Buddhism, Christianity, Hinduism, Taoism, the list can go on. I have been sitting with what the communality is that they share. It is the reliance on the mind and the mind's self-created beliefs. Another communality is its central purpose (I truly believe) to foster a state of love. That said however, any prescribed doctrine is limited because of its prescription, construction, and basis on thought. There are also direct experiences that enter into the equation through one's walk on any specific spiritual path. However, due to the limiting nature of the mind, one can only attain that state which ultimately falls short of sitting in the ultimate essence of who we really are. I say this because any state of being, no matter how wonderful it may feel, electric and charged with the vibrancy of joy and peace it may be, is still being observed by the Divine presence that we are. What do I mean by that? Some of you may have a puzzled look on your faces, right now. I am saying *'that'* which is able to identify that you are having a wonderful 'spiritual' experience, is the ultimate reality... *'That'* is the Real You. If the *Experience* itself were you, there would be nothing aware that you were having an experience. Some Being has to report how you are feeling. That witness of your feeling state is you - is God.

Now, let us pause for a moment right here, because I

know there are certain ones who follow doctrine such as Christianity who may be appalled that I am saying we are God. Other religions may not have such an issue with that statement, such as Hinduism for example; which states that we are God in human form. Whether a doctrine supports that statement or rallies against it doesn't really matter, because the support or non-support is simply another thought form, originating from the mind. Now I do not want to paint the mind as a horrible thing, because it is not. After all, the mind is the faculty through which we maneuver and move through this physical plane. It is however, extremely powerful and seductive in its ability to hypnotize us, placing us under a convincing spell of complete identification with the body, mind, and personality.

A good example of this is the following story. A particular King suffered from amnesia. When reaching adulthood, he abandoned his riches and his kingdom, and he began to travel as a homeless vagrant on the roads throughout town begging for food and places to lay his head. When people who were familiar with who he was in truth would see him, they would say to him, "King, what are you doing?! Why are you begging like this? Don't you know who you are?! You are the King?!!" And of course the King would look at them incredulously, as if they had grown another head in front of his eyes, calling them insane for suggesting that he was in fact "the King"/ (God). Such is the power of the mind in its' complete obscuring of our true Divine nature from us. The irony is it derives power from the very consciousness that it has forgotten it is! Hence, perhaps we can say that the goal of any spiritual path is to realize our true Divine nature, to wake up from the spell that the mind / personality has cast upon us.

I once had a potent experience with being in the presence of people who identified with the Christian faith. While it was a touching, heart-moving experience, it simultaneously left me feeling heavy in my being. It puzzled me how such a heart-connected experience could also leave me feeling weighed down as well. After having sat with it, and spent time meditating, I felt the lightness of being that I have come to experience when the mind, personality, and ideology (basically "thought"), are not present. That is when it hit me. When the mind is not involved, we are simply pure being.

Moreover, while the experience I had of being in the presence of love's energy that weekend was powerful, it was overlain with a particular "belief system". In this case it was Christianity, but it could have been Buddhism or any other" ism". The point is that it was one-step removed from Essence. How could it not be? Thought had entered in. Belief entered. 'Should' and 'should not' entered. History and stories of experiences entered. Labels and judgments, both positive and/or negative, entered. All are thought-based. These are the minds' constructs severing our connection to our true selves... to consciousness. In truth, it is more accurate to say the mind temporarily blinds us to our original nature in that moment. This is truly what I feel the Bible scripture refers to when it speaks of removing the scales from our eyes, as well as "being born again", meaning to be re-born to the truth of our original nature. We are here on the planet to wake up from a mind-induced coma that millions of us suffer from day in and day out. The dream state in which we believe we are, Tanya, African-American, lesbian, female, born in Washington, D.C., personality. You fill in your labels, and thus begins the play of consciousness.

In this moment, I take a new breath, and am born again to the truth that we are infinite and Divine. SoHam!

Essence

You call it chafing the wheat to get to the seed, that process of labeling good, bad, right and wrong,

There are even spiritual chants and songs that speak to the heart of human existence.

Yet with the endless dogma, rules and regulations, there's always something missing

Missing because no amount of well-meaning, belated, best wishes of holy purification, forgiveness of sins, blessings waiting in abundance, stored in heavenly treasures

Can hold a candle next to the effervescent light internally lit that we call the Soul.

Even that name has its limitations because try as one may, it does not capture the essence of the consciousness within which the all is contained.

From animal to flower petal and yes even within that faint whisper of dust, remains the holographic memory that never knew separation from God the Immortal, Infinite bliss,

Until we as humans made it such.

DIARY NOTES

_____

_____

_____

_____

_____

_____

_____

_____

_____

_____

_____

_____

DIARY NOTES

_____

_____

_____

_____

_____

_____

_____

_____

_____

_____

_____

DIARY NOTES

DIARY NOTES

STATE OF NO MIND

If only we remain in the state of 'no memory', we could touch God...that which we are, no textures or colors, yet all textures and colors are encased within the whole as well. Concepts, thoughts, and images flutter through the vast space of our being; and then like ethers, they dissolve back into the substratum of our being. If the illusory nature of this world were revealed, we would have pure vision; a vision that pierces the veil of what we call 'Reality'. These eyes would know no limitation, because they are the eyes of God, housed in this temporary wood frame that we call a body. If only we could maintain the state of non-remembering, pain would cease and any fragments of history would vanish along with the wounding and suffering that has held us prisoner for so long. In that moment we would realize there truly is no "person" to hold prisoner. When we sit in the state of non-remembering, we sit in Pure Being. Let there be no confusion about who we are from this place, because it is not a place. There are no degrees of separation from others to consider. The scales on our eyes fall away and we see only one... Consciousness permeates and is All! This is the state of Non-Remembering...this is the stateless state, because it is simply you and I... synonymous with God.

DIARY NOTES

_____

_____

_____

_____

_____

_____

_____

_____

_____

_____

_____

_____

DIARY NOTES

DIARY NOTES

DIARY NOTES

SEEKER

I have used the word 'seeker' a lot. I am a seeker, spiritual seeker, seeker of truth. I have used it, you have used it. We have all used it in some way, shape, or form. The question dawned on me the other day, "Just what am I seeking?" At that moment, I sat, looking at my surroundings, trying to capture and hold on to a sense of being present to everything and everyone that was with me in that moment. What I felt was a sense of being a part of and disconnected from everything at the same time. Although I saw inanimate objects in front of me and in my periphery, as well as heard voices and sounds, it all felt surreal. Everything was held in the spacious vacuum of my being.

Yet, simultaneously, there was a sense of being the presence that was aware of that feeling, the feeling of wide-opened spaciousness. However, when I consider the question of what I am seeking from this position of viewing everything unfolding within me, it becomes a mute point. I say mute, because everything is contained within me and simultaneously witnessed by 'me'. Therefore, to seek, there has to be an end goal, meaning there has to be an ending point where we discover or find that which we seek. Aaahhh! However, the seeker and the object sought are one! There is such a felt sense of relief from the incessant, compulsive need to obtain something perceived to be separate from ourselves; in its place, resounding peace is left.

Perhaps, the mind convinces us that we are seeking, when in truth we are awakening to who we are and have always been. The illusory nature of this existence is engulfing, and so incredibly powerful in its pull of complete and utter identification with this world. Under its hypnotic perfume, we are left spellbound, enraptured, and completely mesmerized with the trappings of... get this, our own design!! Yes, even the delusion is 'us'! Nothing, nothing is separate from that spacious presence, God, consciousness, I. This is the essence of the bible scripture "I am that I am". How could it be any different? That which is sought and the seeker are one in the same. Therefore, in truth, there is no need to seek... you are already found. Simply pierce the veil and see!

No Words Needed...

Do you realize that there are no words spoken that can express the beauty inherent within you?

There is no phrase, deep contemplation, or expression of thought that reveals the hidden treasure of the essence of your divine being.

Realizing this, give pause for a moment and simply breathe.........

In that breath exists thousands of worlds un-enumerated

Beings float within this cosmic soup un-inebriated

No need for a chemical high

You are the high that you seek!

You are the richness in the bounty that is due to unfold.

We pose for many pictures and Polaroid snapshots of the perfect idealized image of ourselves

Hoping that it will stick!

Not realizing that the picture is only covering a beauty that is deep, rich and too immense to ever be captured by a mere

Illusory snapshot!

Words cannot express this truth.

They are but empty vessels

Carrying hollowed sounds like clanging symbols

Falling on deaf ears.

Our deepest fear is that

Upon quieting of all that noise,

We may disappear.

Truth is, in the moment that we meet the reverberation of the silent waves untethered by our unconscious

Alphabet soup,

There exists an intensity of presence that leaves anyone in its wake completely still

Deeply rooted in that same essence within themselves

No words needed

No voice is flowing

No toning required

No speeches rendered

And yet

You stand

Present!

Full!

Still.

Powerful!

Grounded.

Speaking volumes without words

DIARY NOTES

DIARY NOTES

DIARY NOTES

DIARY NOTES

EXPERIENCE YOUR TRUE SELF

What would remain if in this very moment, you allowed yourself to look? Look at your thoughts, feelings/sensations you are experiencing in your body, emotions that may be arising in you at this very second...try it now. Just keep watching anything that arises within you as if you are watching a movie at the cinema. What do you feel? Focus your attention on any sensations, warmth, tingling, tightness, coolness, and vibrations that you may feel in your body. Now shift your awareness to the in and out ebb of your breath, feeling the coolness of it as it enters your nostrils, flowing down your throat, filling your chest cavity and now your belly. Can you sense yourself becoming broader, more spacious, limit-less? Can you find a boundary? Can you find a place where you begin or end? Who is the one that is watching everything that is "happening"? Who is this witness of the human play unfolding?

Does this watcher have a form, gender, race, or color? Does it have a sexual orientation, a religious belief system, political ideology, educational status/degree, or socio-economic status? Do not regurgitate an answer from what you've heard or read somewhere in a theological or philosophical book. Rather, simply pause, breathe, sit and look... really look. Look without expectation of a particular outcome, but more with open curiosity and a willingness to experience the truth of who you really are.

Are you looking? Thoughts will come, watch them as well, but you simply remain the unattached witness of them, present and simply looking at the movie that is playing out in front of you.

Now ...question...

Who are you?

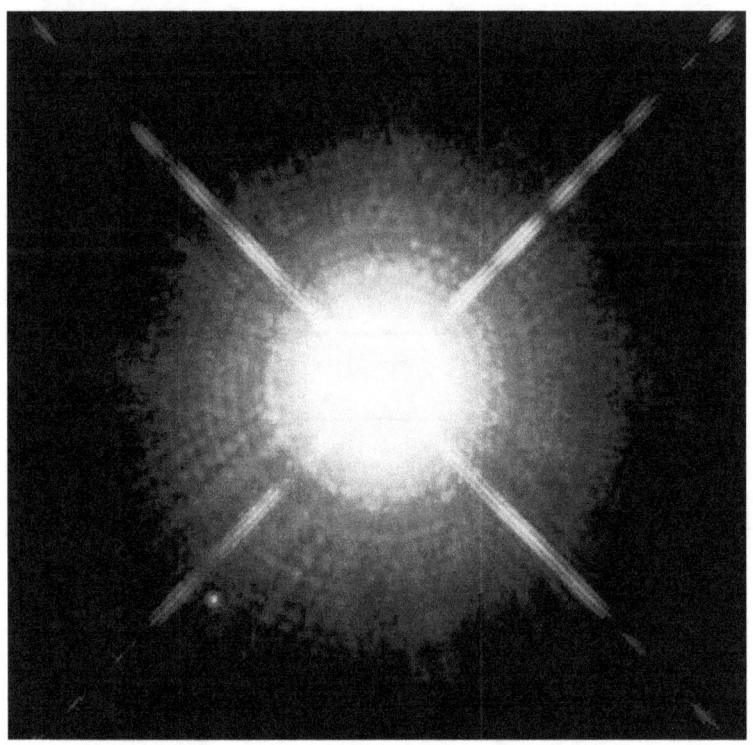

DIARY NOTES

_____

_____

_____

_____

_____

_____

_____

_____

_____

_____

_____

_____

DIARY NOTES

DIARY NOTES

DIARY NOTES